FOREVER AFTERNOON

LOTUS POETRY SERIES
Naomi Long Madgett, Senior Editor

Books by Adam David Miller:
Dices or Black Bones, ed.
Neighborhood and Other Poems
Forever Afternoon

FOREVER AFTERNOON

Poems by
Adam David Miller

Michigan State University Press
East Lansing
1994

Copyright © 1994 by Adam David Miller

All Michigan State University Press books are produced on paper which meets the requirements of American National Standard of Information Sciences— Permanence of paper for printed materials ANSI Z39.48-1984.

Michigan State University Press
East Lansing, Michigan 48823-5202

02 01 00 99 98 97 96 95 94 1 2 3 4 5 6 7 8 9

Library of Congress Cataloging-in-Publication Data

Miller, David Adam
    Forever afternoon : poems / Adam David Miller.
        p.   cm. — (Lotus poetry series ; 2)
  ISBN 0-87013-354-3
  I. Title. II. Series.
PS3563.I37414F67 1994
811'.54—dc20
                                       94-3903
                                          CIP

To Carmen, Robin and Pemba

CONTENTS

ACKNOWLEDGMENTS

Thanks to the San Francisco East Bay poetry community, especially coffee houses, the galleries and workshops, and Pacifica Radio's KPFA that provided constructive forums for the reading of many of these poems.

Thanks to the Ina Coolbrith Poetry Circle's Ina Graham Award for "Body-snatchers," a first prize in their Short Poems category.

Special thanks to my editorial committee of Mary Berg, Jannie Dresser, Henrietta Harris, and Elise Peeples; and to Lotus Poetry Series editor Naomi Long Madgett, whose close reading of the manuscript has made it a better book.

As winner of the first Naomi Long Madgett Poetry Award, my thanks to the judges and the Hilton-Long Poetry Foundation.

— *A.D.M.*

MORNING MANTRA

Morning means re-ordering aches and grimaces.
Mostly it's swivel parts and knees.
Four fingers of right hand hold my body

hostage. Pain streaks through them to neck
and the twitch in shoulder starts a dance.
Mind says get up, get up. Six o'clock,

day's waiting. But body: "Hey, I need
a jump start, a brand new heart. A pig's foot
and a bottle of beer or two." Unh unh, naw,

maybe an aspirin or so will have to do.
When I finish smiling at the silliness
in my life, false starts, fizzled ends,

I stretch to see if back cooperates,
massage where it joins the rest of me,
oooomm my morning mantra: Get your bottom up now,

get your bottom up, now. Despite the creak
of dry bones dry bones that know nothing
of gentilesse, I do.

Forever Afternoon

What is death to the caterpillar
we call a butterfly
— anon.

Ladder of success is an image I abhor
I prefer the double helix, intertwining spirals.

My spirit does not wear down
or wear out, like a car or a shoe.

While my body wanes, waxes my spirit brighter.

I am in eternal metamorphosis.
Constantly consumed,
I consume myself.

Life has no stages; the word resolution
lies; life has questions, connections.

Life is a wheel of fortune, my life
a gift to be passed around the wheel.

Do we ask where does the caterpillar
go when it becomes a butterfly?

The caterpillar does not go, it becomes.

Spirit of caterpillar lives in butterfly,
same heart, beating stronger.

FINEST SHOES

Aged nine years already my feet took
a small man's shoe. "Steamboats,"
my companions derided. "Battleships," I countered.

That Carolina winter I walked to school
barefoot, bragging hollowly that my boats
were tougher than my schoolmates
whose shoes had soles on them.

Widowed and wizened, Mrs. Gissentana
saw me pass her house.
Explosive, five-two like my mother,
alert to her young neighbor's plight.

Came to our house with hands
in her apron. "That boy feet cold."
"He want to go to school."
"What you go do, you go let him freeze?"
"I'mmo put *me* on his feet?"

Alone, burdened with four (rheumatic
fever hadn't freed my other sister yet)
under twelve, what was she to do?

"I'mmo take him with me to Silver's."
My mother threw a look at me,
saw my eagerness to go down town.
Tear proud she nodded her agreement.

Mr. Silver (changed from Silverstein) sold
used clothing from New York. Noticing
Mrs. Gissentana examining a pair
of walking shoes, he hurried over.

"My boy,
back to college
left these
hardly worn
75 cents too much?"

Mrs. Gissentana snorted.

My finest shoes had been worn
by a small Jewish man.

The Postman Rang for Us

He was "our" mailman.

Fifteen white folk worked
in the post office,
he the only colored
except the janitor.

No, he delivered mail to white folks, too.
He was making swings
when white men were in the back room
playing monopoly
and when they had retired
for the day.

Six straight times he was at the top
of the civil service list.
An inspector had to come down
from Washington before they hired him.
Drew a government check then,
they couldn't mess with that.

Should think his wife would have been
proud of him, and perhaps she was.
But the man who ran the lumberyard
got any woman in town he wanted
(or so it was said).

Beaten down by mail sacks
and a wife who cheated,
our mailman hung in his job,
whistled on his rounds,
sent a daughter away to college,
and basked in our praise.

MY MOTHER WANTED GOOD FOR ME

I learned to fix shoes,
loving the smell of leather
and the look on people's faces
when their shoes were neat.

But counters were not my meat.
I've never liked to sell.
Something in the grasping side
of folk I'd rather not see.
Maybe it's my own grasping
I turn from,
that lurking greed in me?
So I left off shoe repair
And went to sea.

My mother wanted me
to have an honest occupation,
like my father and stepfather before me.
Seafaring to her was lower than busting rock.
At houses she'd worked were signs:
"Sailors and dogs keep off the grass."

I couldn't carry my mother around
in my head or in my pocket;
nor could I be what my father
or stepfather had been.
She nor I had ever seen the ocean.
I had read that salt air was good
for lots of things. As I slipped
into my peacoat and pulled down
my watch cap,
I told her that.

La Mouche

I will kill you, fly, though you don't bother me.
You bother her and she bothers me.
"Get it out of here! There is
one buzzing around. I saw it
come in."

If she said you brought in filth, I'd
understand it. I don't like filth myself,
but there's no filth in our backyard.

Is it because you're black and make noise,
and look sometimes like a bee?

I don't want to kill you, you don't bother me.
She bothers me. She screeches my life out.

Perhaps we can join forces. You lie quiet.
Then one day when she turns her back
we'll both buzz away.

WATCHING THE FLEA CIRCUS SHE THOUGHT

Watching the fleas
the little girl thought,
why not find the right pitch
for the fleas, the best tone,
the right rhythm?
Make them dance; free up
the dogs and cats;
keep them dancing,
dance themselves silly,
and then die happy.

CHAMELEON

Mancha Cat
thinks he's a dog.
He will chase and fetch
fetch and carry
catch and carry.

He never misses

till he changes his mind.
Then he becomes a cat again
and ignores the toy I throw
as it soars over his head.

Looks at me as though he's
saying, "I'm a cat.
Didn't you know?"

CATTALK

Neighborhood cats hold their parliament
on the flat roof of our garage; it is
their throne room, their sanctum sanctorum,

refuge from pine cones I throw
when they anoint my vegetable garden.
Early morning sun catches them

in their cleansing ritual, licking
away at legs and sides. The meow meows
congregate and a chicken wire fence

protects them. Heat inflames the tar and gravel.
Not a paw raised in dissent
as each adjourns to a corner in the shade.

Running Away

I'll skip, I'll skip with the jumping rope
I'll ride the merry train,
I'll trot away on the tumbledown horse
But I won't come back again.

I'll run run run to the end of the road
Where the sky plummets down to the sea,
And I'll take my squirrel with me
Where the sky drops down to the sea.

I'll crik crik crik
Like a cricket in a crack
But I won't come back.

And he'll be sad when he finds me gone
Because I've warned him times before,
If he didn't stop it I'd run away
To the land with the farthest shore.

I'll hit the dusty trail,
Slap, flap, with the flat of my feet.

I'll fly, I'll fly, over the highest hill,
Where the moon makes a hole in the sky,
And I'll take my squirrel with me,
Where the moon makes a hole in the sky.

I'll trot away on the tumbledown horse
I'll ride the merry train,
If my father ever spanks me anymore,
I won't come home again.

IN HOMAGE TO THE BLACK FIG*

Planting is an act of faith.
Planting a tree is a step
to renew the earth. Planting
a fig tree instills the body
with spirit.

Our spirit is in this tree.
Mia, your spirit is in this tree.
Your spirit is in this tree, Stefan.
Michelle, your spirit is in this tree.
Chloe, your spirit is in this tree.
Your spirit is in this tree, Valerie.
Zoe, your spirit is in this tree.

The arms of the fig stretch around the earth
as does your gene pool: Asia Minor, ·
The Americas, Africa, Europe.
The fig is an old old food, of many
colors: green, brown, black.

Dressed as a fig
was once to be gaudy.

Were you the fruit Eve chose?
Fig, whose royal succulence
ripened in sun, juices tautly held,
do you give freely to all who pluck?

Small is this tree, as you are small now,
but you won't be small always.

As the fig will grow, absorbing
rain and sun, so will you grow,
soaking up sun and rain.
I shall tend the tree, your parents' love
will sustain you.

One day I will see you gather,
arms around its trunk, sing,
dance, and enjoy the ancient food.

The black fig will be waiting,
leaves green, branches flush; for now,
spread connected as you are to the points of stars.

---

* The black fig was planted to celebrate my two grands, my wife's niece, and children of two friends.

AFTER THE PARTY

My guests keep me human.
I see myself in them, them in me.
When they come, bringing food and laughter,
they cheer me. I love
when they dance, talk loud and long,
or sit quietly in groups.

I pleasure myself in their eyes,
I absorb their richness,
their roses, their thorns.

I am less without my guests.
A chaff blowing, they anchor me.

By entering a space so precious to me,
my guests make real time of party time,
tipping the cornucopia of their love
in my direction.

On Her Birthday

— *to M.T.N.*

I cannot find a totem for you,
having combed the animal,
plant and mineral kingdoms
and come up empty.

Perhaps the spirit world,
double of our own, will let go
a proper shadow to reflect on.

How is it that you escape definition?
Are your limits so vast
they evade detection?

Not that I would encompass you,
but the many qualities of your face
stun me. Their multiple shades
constantly create new distinctions.

Miracle of oneness,
we are so easy together,
circle within circles,
world within worlds.

THE ANNIVERSARY

They say one has to be a little mad
to marry.
There must have been times
you wanted to call it quits
but you didn't,
times you wondered *why*.

"Till death do us part":
Powerful words, uttered only
by the young or foolish.
They say one has to be
a little mad to marry.

Sometimes it is good
to simply live long enough,
balancing 'store with loss' and loss with gain.

To stay married you go beyond love.
You learn to change
and accept change.

It is always a modest joy
we end up with.

FIVE GREEN YEARS

Even after you returned my bond
and said, "I'll stay," we
still didn't know how long.
"As long as love lasts." Not a stable
basis for a marriage. For
an affair. Yes. Perfect for that.
Peculiar madness, love. But
we've survived five green years
and thrived. Economy in the black,
blue days at a minimum.
We are new people. We love
with passion. Gold glow in warm dark.

To Shiro-San on His Seventieth

— to S.N.

Let us sing glad songs to Shiro-San,
a man with a life rich and whole.

Age dulls the memory of pain,
renders the barbed wire, gun towers,
two-lane fog shrouded road to work
at five in the morning, bearable,
all for the sake of the family.
The sun blends with the shade.

Years of sun and shade,
magical hands that weld a family,
the cycle of memory and loss,
the fact of flesh and its claim;
all driven by a formidable heart.

It fits you well, the dignity of age,
like a suit stamped with pride;
your eyes that see through lives,
looking into the forever sun.

In Memoriam: Ted Cunningham (1926-1971)

> It is said
> A man is not dead
> As long as he lives
> In the minds of his friends.
> — *African Peoples' Story*

Ted
He dead
Preacher said
Our eyes red
From crying

Death surprises
We can go
Death surprises
We can't know
Death surprises
Any time now
Death realizes
Any time then

You came to us out of the Church.
When you set aside your order
and joined with a woman who had set
aside hers, it was no idle act. You
had both tried, worked and prayed.
Been rewarded and paid your share.

You were early in an exodus
many hoped would teach the Church
something. Did you know then
that Camerounais Bernard Fonlon was defrocked
for protesting unequal treatment
of African priests?

Though you left your order, you never left
the spiritual life. You loved music
and growing things. You soared on wings
of Trane, Dizzy, Bud, had flights with SunRa,
Nina, Duke and the high priests MJQ:
a cathedral of spirit, these sounds.

Hardly had you tested your new life,
enjoyed your wife, child, new work, friends
when the cancer that claimed you struck
its discordant note.

Happy Morning Man,* we are bereft.
What could we have done
to keep you here among us?
How will we assuage ourselves
for your loss?

> Ted he dead
> Tipped away
> Always expecting
> That we can go
> Any of us
> At any time
> For any reason
> For no reason
> 'Time and chance'
> Happens to us all.

---

* From Al Young, *Geography of the Near Past.*

PRAISE, PRAISE MUSIC

Music reaching a sky free of sky-gods
Music of the earth
    From the earth
    Metals from the mines
    Reeds from the fields
    From the woods roll the drums
Praise the folk, praise Four Blind Boys

Praise Grover Washington, Jr., praise Bach,
    Kent Nagano, Jon Jang, Anthony Davis,
    Buffy St. Marie, Ali Akbar Khan,
    Quila Pajun, Inti-Illimani

A.K. Black who played a sky-god
in Benjamin Britten's *Noah* —
who rapped an "Introduction to Destruction"
that blew us all away. Praise eco-rap!

Laurie Anderson, John Cage, Frank Zappa

Rosalyn Tureck is Ms. Bach, but I heard her
with my own ears stomp out a boogie woogie.
Praise Bach, praise Boogie Woogie.

Hey baba lee bop! Hey baba lee bop!
Praise the folk, praise Kitka,
Praise Howling Wolf and Bartok and Duke

    Nancy Wilson
    Went to town
    Riding on a pony
    Stuck a feather in her hair
    And Hey, now!

This body, this tube out of which
miraculous sounds pour; O miracle
this body

    Clap your hands
    Beat your thighs
    Slap your chest
    Stomp your feet

Listen to the sounds, listen to the music, yes
Oh clap your hands, whenever you want to
Clap your hands whenever you want to

    Praise music
    Praise music
    Praise

THE HIT

I have to write a thousand lines
for each ten I can keep.

In film work they shoot seven to get one;
one hit in three tries makes a fine hitter.

I should work where the odds
are not so long, you say, to sing my song.

Perhaps I would be a sweet swinger,
my stroke a thing of beauty;
or snap the picture
a thousand words can't match, natch!
Or maybe not be so fussy.

But when we scream in ecstasy
at the hit over the left field fence,
or admire the photograph on the gallery wall,
behind them are the wasted many thousands —

"Two thousand at bats," I
was told, "against big league pitching,
to become a hitter."

"For that one," she said, "that one on the wall there,
I don't know." And she waved her hands
in the direction of infinity.

So better for me I should stick to words,
be fussy, pick them clean and pick them fine.

DIANE'S INN

She opens her heart
and her space
to us,
we who would be poets,
lovers, gods.

With a face that flashes welcome
she makes us feel wanted.
We think we can be somebody;
I shine, you shine, we all shine.

Our rhymes and meters,
mirrors of lives
that hang at the edge of the real,
lance our festering loneliness
as we gather there
and she listens.

In Age, One Sorrow

I understand your jealousy,
                    my friend,
wild like Scythians,
simmering like the Moor.

I, too, see hands younger,
newer than mine, fairer than mine,
turn handkerchiefs into delicacies
                    like steel,
wreathed in winged laurel,

while I, rope muscled,
tugging through the ink of hours,
work a dead end.

Young hands, newer, fairer by far,
soar like falcons,
                    while I sit
mired in ems and blanked copy,
feather nested duckling turned gander.

Command Performance

Raised surfaces, shapes burned from tin,
Sand blasted stone to make a figure in,
Words that tell what the body does in secret,
Unleashed acetylene.

Our minds, encoursed from fish to nebulae,
From atoms to atoms, give pause
To make this astounding definition;

We were commanded by the idiom first of all to *see*,
Seduced by Joyce into being revealed,
Forced by Ginsberg's *Howl* and Kerouac to feel.

At the Park

Yeats among his school children swings
gates open to endless speculation,
the child, man, forever questioning
what to know.

As the ball bounces, which is bouncer,
which is bounce?

We swing on a gateless gate, open,
open to a dark ring skittering,
skittering in the droppings of a bird.

Camus Meursault and his sublime indifference,
equal to that of the universe,
S. Crane and his universe who did not care.
Equal to Macleish's tall tent, equal
to the roof of the world blown whoof.
A tiny rent in Christendom?

God!

The myriad ways of saying nothing,
nothing, nothing . . . nothing at all.

THE GARDEN

There is satisfaction in turning earth,
A measured amount to accomplish,
One forkful at a time,
Preparing a place to plant.

Adds up before you know it:
Earth turned, composted, weeds under,
Muscling the fork in, quick twist of the wrists,
You can see what you've done.

Earth's there to receive the seed,
Nothing abstract or subjective, no caprice.
The judgment of the land is absolute.
Just running sweat under the sun
And a prayer for cooling rains.

LIMANTOUR

From my back in the dunes,
Engorging the roar and the wash,
Eyes closed but for the shimmer world,
Half light on my lashes,
Winds cool the sun on my face.
With a single pant, a dog crashes by.

Sophocles and Matthew Arnold heard
This roar, and my uncle Benjamin?
No, only I,

The interminable cry of gulls soaring,
Swerving, beating and calling, beating
Against the wind or riding it.

The sea rolls out past Maui,
Past New Caledonia, to Durban.
Winter solstice, closing down, storing up.

Sounds edge between boom
And wash.
Is there a sob under the roar?

It is a winter's beach, water bright sand.
Ocean, a lazy green, launches wave
Upon wave, the retreating and returning sea.

The sky is a page to be written on.

PT. REYES FAULT

Gulls working the wind,
eyeless Cheshire cat fish heads
on the beach as the two push upwind
against swirling sands.

-This bit of land here
 was once 500 miles south.
–It was?
–Yes, moving north at one centimeter a year.
–You mean that where we're walking
 was once in Tijuana?
–Just about. See, there's granite here.
 None just over the hill, she said.
–Oh, he said.
 You mean those masks that look
 like animals at a meeting?
–Yes, she said.
–Oh, he said.
 Then a hole could open up right here,
 a chasm we couldn't leap across?
She smiled,
–The fault's right up the sand there.

Wind and waves
fight eternally for control of the beach,
sea against land.

–Lots of people build on faults.
 I used to live on one.
–How did it feel? he asked.
–No different from any other place,
 only you never knew
 when you'd wake up
 with your bed in your bathtub
 and your bathtub

in your neighbor's garage.
—You think you're smart,
you know that, don't you?
She didn't answer him but kicked
beach sand savagely as they walked.

Sand piper runs ahead of wave,
leaps up when surprised,
follows wave out, picking, picking.

COMFORT STATION #473-1

Comfort station
number four-seven-three dash one
is for me a Free Zone
for early morning fancy
in Lassen Volcanic National Park.

Its stately high seat
brings the ceiling down.
Colored light strains through.

My tinted pee beats pastel drops
from a tinted penis
against a tinted forewall.

Four-seven-three is a Siamese twin,
as water falling below
next door reminds me of our
joint disposal system.

I hear my neighbor
grunt and sigh and rain down pee.
This pleasing duet,
muted underground, is a
product of modern design
and a unisex morality.

I wonder what she thinks of me
as we struggle through our morning emptying.

O Styrofoam and plastic wonder,
with your cement base
and translucent circle in your ceiling,
there is nothing natural about you
except us sitting, sitting.

Yet, since a morning seat
is for contemplation
not perturbation,
I salute you.

You furnish assembly line jobs
for workers in Torrance,
freight for Southern Pacific
and a place of relief
for us two.

WAITING OUTSIDE THE CLUB

I watch the water running down
off roof, down windshield,
water running down, time running down.

She parks in the space
one over from mine,
in the car her parents gave her,
so that she has her own wheels
at parties.

She looks over at me
then down.
I turn away
when she sees me watching.

I listen to gospel,
smug in my car;
she smug in her car, Top 40 blaring.

We are trapped in rain,
    in cars,
trapped in gospel,
    Top 40's,
trapped in time,
trapped in lives
waiting to swim

THOUGHTS ON THE SIX-THIRTY A.M. SWIM

The early morning genie
rises above the splaish splaish
serious dolphins humping.
Wind skips the water scattergreen.

There is something psychological about the wall
both goal and barrier, help and hindrance.
Flip at twenty-five, touch at fifty
breathe at one hundred.
I want a stream, the bay, the ocean
I want freedom.

Wind skips the water scattergreen.

I compete against myself,
arm around the board, watch on wrist
my feet a gyro
kicking like an Evenrude.
Suck out my marrow, fill my bones with air.
I push me beyond where I was.

What is water?

Of the five senses, they say
there is only one sense, of touch.
All is touch.
You touch the water, scoop, scull.

Controlling the pool is power,
power and grace, sculling, sculling.

Breathing is easier when you've done
the first hundred meters. Such peace, backstroke;
pull, glide after a sprint.

There are no straight lines in swimming.
There are no straight lines in swimming.

You're doing the breaststroke,
pennants whipped horizontal.

Wind skips the water scattergreen.

You wonder, "What am I doing here?"
Raindrops freeze as they fall, and prick your back.
Then you know why you are here:
You're a fool, an utter fool,
one who loves water, is one with it.
For water is air and earth and fire.

So the five senses are only touch.
So the elements are only water.
Everything partakes of it,
even breath.

BE MY LOVE

You asked for rain, I brought thunder.
You asked about tomorrow and I shied away
from predictions. I could handle today,
but who would follow the unknown?

Nestmaker, your search was for land
and a protected space.
I, herder, put my faith in cattle and dreams.

Like rails we were, switched by fate
and that turn in our lives, into a crossing.
Crossing we joined and traveled a short way together,
but like rails, again we sprung apart.

I needed the woman in you then, to cement
the man in me. What you needed was

not protection, really. You knew at base
your bulwark was yourself. You needed,
as you said, a partner to join you in the dance.

But I, no mean dancer, could not hack it.
You were too many for me, too many
and too swift, your turkey in the straw
too much for my slow drag.

LOVE POEM

We don't have to plan love.
It is in our talk
of vacuum cleaning
or fixing a broken zipper.

Loving is not to break stride
but to do what there is to do.
We don't have to work at love
but at cooking dinner
and hanging the wash.

Exchanging events in our lives,
we do what we do
as we do it, as natural as breathing.
You smell like sunshine wash.
Sunshine turns me around
and around and around.

When You Come, When Will You Come

Will you come when the wind is screaming?
Will you come in the rain?
Will you come when the rain is falling,
Will you come in the wind?

Who needs you as a sunshine baby?
Everybody's coming then.
The sun brings us all together,
In the fields, at the beach, at the inn.

Will you come in the rain, my baby,
Will you come in the wind?
Don't need you as a sunshine baby,
Don't need you as a sunshine baby.

For You Alone

A friend of mine said once,
to look at the back of Adam Clayton
Powell at a table
excited her beyond imagining.

To see your back there,
charmed by that talk,
your mind elsewhere,
changed the glow from the skylight,
made me sing sweet songs.

I could feel your voice change
when you heard me enter.
Though you said nothing to me,
all you spoke was for my ears,
what I did was for your ears,

my sounds, my silences,
my song.

A Hole in My Night

There's a hole in my night
and the wind is screaming.

I've been trying to plug that hole
but the moon ain't right.

There's a hole in my night.
Not the kind that sheep race through;
it's bigger than that.
I pull down my hat,
put hands to my ears
to block out the screams.

Keep telling myself
I must be dreaming.
Wake up in the morning,
hole's not there.
My days are whole,
but there is a hole, a hole, a hole,
a hole in my night.

STOLEN PEACE AT WINDOVER

So peaceful here, she said.
Yes, he sighed.
They looked down over red roofs.
Breeze pressed against her face
through a crack in the window.
They looked at the black pine
and clouds that scraped the bay.

Their minds turned to their worlds outside.
Her hand in his grew limp.
"I shan't come again."
It has been peaceful here, he said.

OH TO HAVE LOVED AND LOST

When you have loved once and only once,
and lost, why is there no act too petty,

no meanness too minute, to spite
the ex-beloved? Why do you need
to see groveling eyes, feel arms
around your knees, seek utter
destruction of the one once treasured?

Is it that you don't want to play
the fool, that you would obliterate
the object of your shame?

Maybe you should love more times
more often. Scatter your joy, spread your loss.
That way you would not need to heap
the burden of your emptiness on any one heart.

With many ex-lovers in your life,
might you even learn
to like them a little?

Reach Out to Touch

Snail trail glistening on the rug,
talking drum squat by the dux chair,
the room's light brackish,
as the boy in the hallway
phones his father about Bob Dylan.

There is this concert coming soon.

The drum silent, 7,000 miles from home,
listens as an alien.

The room's light brackish
as the boy in the hallway

I know you gave me the watch and jacket,
I appreciate it.

Talking drum squat by the dux chair

only none of my buddies are into leather,
I mean, I am grateful for your gifts.

It's just that, yes, my Mom and Mike treat me fine;
I wondered if *you* would like to go
see Bob Dylan with me.

The room's light brackish

They bought me a ticket — Busy? I mean, I understand.
I'm sorry. I'm sure. Yes, I understand.

The room's light brackish,
talking drum squat by the dux chair,
snail trail glistening on the rug,
the boy talking, talking.

THE GALILEANS

Two common criminals
and a political prisoner,
that's how they think it was.

Well, I was up there
because they said I stole something.
Nothing political about that.

Cat was not much whiter than I was.
Came on talking all that off the wall stuff,
like, the meek shall inherit the earth.
Then he'd contradict himself,

the poor shall always be with you.
Well, I didn't take no always being poor.

I'd always worked hard, *hard*,
in the fields, the mines, on the waterfront.

No matter how much or how hard I worked,
I never got out from under.

I make it, taxes get it.
Tried share cropping, landlord take it.
Had kids to feed; kept my nose clean
till then.

Have you seen Appian Way?
See any rich men on them crosses?
They're all poor like me, and black or brown,
or crazies like him they call political.

Cat tried to 'save' me for his God.
Hell, I wanted to be cut down.
Now, is that political or what?

I would have followed the cat,
I mean, if he really wanted to stone get down
and tear the mother up, but he didn't.
He was only into just some jive time reforms.
Judas had the right idea.
Like it wasn't a color, it's a system.

I'm not a snitch or nothing,
I wouldn't have fingered the cat;
but he was talking trash, *trash*,
and I for damn sure couldn't go where he led.

BROKEN RECORD

Nobody's waiting for me,
nobody's expecting me.
This morning's like yesterday
and the day before.
No one will phone me
or come by.

If I go to their house, they won't know
what to do with me.

Stand me up against a wall
and look at me.

Why should anyone come by here?
They've got nothing to bring me.
My friends, like me,
they're empty handed, dust in their pockets;
even the hustles are slimming down
and getting brutal. Why should I
wake up, try to bounce out,
dance on around? Around where?
You tell me. I have done all that.
Have been there and back.

I had a little job. Six years.
Got me a car, some furniture,
and a TV. Doing all right.
Had even thought about getting
married. Ooooh! I was luckyee
to escape that. At least
I didn't add no empty mouths
or pinched stomachs.

But I'd like to marry, least
to live with someone. That way

we could help one another
start to build up something.

The sun's shining out there. California sun.
The sun's always shining in California.
But it's a hard sun, it don't mean
anything for anybody I know.

I'd rather have storms, steel winds,
sleet against my face, the way I feel.
You can fight that —

When they laid me off, all of us
that had come in at the end, I asked
when I could expect to be back.
They said the downturn in the economy
was on the upswing.
Inflation was being checked
and the recession was receding.
Then they told me to pick up my two weeks.

That was a year ago.

I can't lay in this bed, the sun
streaking in the window like that.
Can't fight the sun, it just shines.
Didn't create all this mess,
mustn't forget that.

I won't fight the sun today.
I'll hang my feet over the side of the bed,
ease them to the floor. Stand up.

They won't call me
I'll have to find my friends,
and go out .

STREET SCENES, 1993

Used to be they
thought we were crazy
Not so hard on us then
Now they say we criminal
Watch out

Checked his blue
flak jacket before
I hung it on the railing
by the post office
Plastic razor, some
cookie crumbs
a plastic dab of mustard
from a fast food joint

Given: the rich get theirs
Given: rest of us scuffle
over what's left

A reporter
came by here
asked me
what was my
vantage point
I said I had
no vantage point

People study us
a lot

Never ask
why we are
poor
We'd ask them
to look in the mirror

Saw that
crippled poet
the other day
She writes poems
about us
Nice to have
someone write poems
about us

Every night
the dark comes
and I'm scared

They spent
more money
trying to find
her people
after she died
than when
she was
hungry

Talk about
the shelters
like they some
heaven
They ever
sleep in one?

WHICH COP WOULD SHOOT A BANKER?
—for Jannie

Standing at my upstairs window,
I saw a man pumping it down the street,
chased by policeman, traffic heavy,
leap and roll over top of car

driven by startled woman; scramble up
and run on. He was gaining,
approaching freedom, when,

"Halt!" and a single shot.

With a look of horror, the woman,
incredulous, stricken, wandered between
man thrashing on sidewalk

holding his smashed leg,
and the puffing policeman
who had called for back-up.

"Anybody got a cigarette? Couldju
give m' wife uh message?" He was not dressed
like a banker.

Neighbors, children who had been playing
in the street, and the driver,
now beside herself, crowded among

the many police. A siren sounded
in the distance. Snatches of talk told
me the shot man was an accused shoplifter.

With all these cops on the loose
there might be other bullets flying.
Even though I was white, neatly dressed
and female, taking no chance,
I stepped away from the window.

Lee Undergoes the Knife

Lee is scheduled to go under
the knife on the thirteenth of April,
wouldn't you know?

We are not superstitious,
but when they are going to cut you open
in April on the thirteenth
you take all the odds you can get.

Don't walk under ladders
on the way to surgery.

Surgery.

"It is not major," they tell us.
"Just a little three-part thing.
At the third phase we do a
biopsy."

Oh.

We each try to keep up
the spirits of the other.

I tell her we're going
to get money back from the IRS.
"That's because we're not making
any," she counters.

"It's nice the house was safe
when we got back from Mexico this year,"
she offers.
(Last year we had been robbed.)

"Now I can get started on some
of the thirteen jobs on my 'to-do' list."
Oops! That number again.

We both know it's going to be
all right.

Surgeons are so clever these days,
the more complicated the operation
the greater their mastery of it.

It's going to be all right.
It's going to be all right.

We believe it will. But we would feel
our odds were ever so much greater
had they told us her surgery
was something major.

THE ASSISTANT

Never seen directly, talked over and around,
first-named by everyone while titles
tinkle their way through the hallways.

You move in tandem with those you work for,
the dance of hands that touch but seldom entwine,
pirouette of eyes.

Your routine is a round: snap to,
set up, look out, help out, take down,
clean up, snap to.

Appreciated but never enough,
guardian of the patient and the space,
cover for things better not to see.

Between you and them they keep a glass wall,
class the secret they enforce by titles
and places you won't be invited.

So you split your mind, the double-bubble,
smile here, frown there: will the children
get to school on time? Will they remember
to triple lock the doors?

COACH RESIGNS TO HUMANITY

I saw my elders cheat to get me,
broke the rules they made.
These were my idols, my main men,

as the black boys say. The rules they broke
were stupid rules, made to be
broken. We all knew that.

Competition was our breath, we
suck on winning. Discipline
was our credo, discipline.

I was a pulling guard, much sought after,
did it right, had the coaching, training,
good high school, small college to big time.

Got my chance to coach when I was
on injured reserve. Liked it so much
I never played again.

You had to go along to get along,
I learned that early. The system
has just so much give. I drink

more than I should. Try to watch it.
Couldn't survive a DUI, not these days
when videotape can zap you.

They don't give you time to think
about anything but what to do next:
the recruiting, rubber chicken circuit

buttering up alumni, the press,
college, the season getting longer.
Even the earth rests in winter. The

system makes it impossible for you
not to cheat. When you're in the public
eye you get called things. Nothing to do

about it but hunker down. Heard
in a philosphy class once a line
that stuck: Unexamined life is not

worth living. The recruiting was what
got to me in the end. Grown men
scrambling after boys. Something

low about it. But it had to be done,
no recruiting, no team. And never
to be Number One. Good group of boys,

schedule too weak; strong schedule,
team bombs. Can't remember last meal
where I ate all my food. My wife asked me

to reconsider. "At fifty-eight you've got
a lot left to offer humanity." I told her
she had a point there.

JOCK SNIFTER

You get your kicks from that?
How they smell, man, how they smell?
— *H.E. Ballso*

When you got nothing to write, you write
anyhow. That's when you create the best:

"He pulled the anterior cruciate
ligament." That about me. Anyone tell you

doctor report might be just that, report?
Hang around the clubhouse, the office

waiting for handouts, like the Washington
Press Corps. The President he burp, they lap

it up. Same thing here. "Coach Lattimer
picks his teeth with a gold toothpick."

How he pick his nose?

We mercenaries, hired guns. When you write
that? You know's well's I do pro sports

pig in a swill pen. (No offense to pigs.)
Wasn't for that court suit by Curt Flood

and the courage of Sandy and Drysdale
I'd still be a slave. We all would.

You say you got to balance your reporting.
You do my big foot. When I'm too hurt to play

you say, "He's dogging it." White cat out
you jump all sympathetic looking for reasons.

I play hurt. We all do. Never know it
from what you write.

Just because I don't go for that super
macho bull, trash talking, don't mean I'm not

"aggressive." I protect myself. But I don't
give myself no bonus points for messing up

a cat's career. He got to eat like me
and feed his family. Mama always told me,

"Can't talk you cuss. I'm teaching you to talk."
I learned to read and write before I got
to college. Glad I did.

Why when I do well, I'm the exception?
White cat do well, it's expected. Why?

Why the white cat's the "thinking" player,
I play by "instinct"? Why? Number one,

what's so wrong with instinct that white cats
don't have none? Number two, don't I bust

my butt in training and weight room and diet?
I play well because I feel shame when I don't.

All Star point guard can't be no fool now,
you better believe it.

You wonder sometime I won't talk to you,
ain't 'cause you white and I'm black,

it's 'cause you're careless and won't listen.
White cats say the same. You have your deadlines

and fans to please, like we have. Granted.
But do check out the difference

between what we say and what you write.
Look as if we never opened our mouths.

Now sleep on that.

THE SQUARE RING

— to Joan Ryan

"You get them in trouble,"
a man told Sugar Ray.
"It's my business
to get them in trouble,"
Sugar Ray told the man.

Hot lights, crowd chanting his name,
adrenalin shoots through his fear.
At the bang of the bell he is alone.
Hands between him, shame and destruction.
Pain he must master, fear he must conceal.

His opponent seeks to thunder
leather on his skull, plunder
him of his senses. Jab, jab, feint,
move, jab, cross, move, *move, move.*
He can't confuse the fake for the blow.

He must draw his opponent in,
lure him, trap him, upset
his timing, break him, make him weep.

Jab, jab, move, feint, cross, jab, move, move.
He knows the ring is not a safe place
for children or the unafraid.

Under the glare of lights, eyes of the crowd,
he is more exposed than the corner back,
goalie, pitcher, point man, blues man,
monologist; he is toreador
with a thinking foe.

As the rounds add, the ring subtracts.
Time expands.
What is that opening he sees? It may
not come again. Entree or snare?
Is this the moment for the left hook?

What are you scheming, trickster man?
One swing away from heaven or from hell.

THE BUS STOPS AT GOLDEN GATE BRIDGE
FOR TOURISTS AND OTHER
INTERESTED PERSONS

Water
Fire and Water
These were the instruments
of your last push

Water and Fire
Water
Water flowing west
to find east
It is that clear and that crazy

And so you
out of water into the flames
tried to fight fire with fire

You
in fire once the waters broke
and flooded you
onto the glass-strewn plain
It was incendiary
tracers glowing seconds
to light the way

And so you
my daughter
who never believed we could love you
shied away from the high places
until that evening
schedule firmly grasped
you leaped into the screaming wind
and ebbing tide

CRACKS IN THE WALL HOLDS FLOWERS

After each quake
new cracks appear in the wall.
These fissures, forced by cataclysm,
hold flowers.

Vast natural damage is
marked always by rumblings
deep in earth maternal. Lilacs breed
and hang in a nook near the edge of the sun.

My uneasiness,
reminded of a niche now brown,
is not soothed by the prospect of flowers.

THE BODYSNATCHERS

Sitting on a quiet day
watching my shadow
as the sun passed over,
a tiny fleck flew out of it
growing ever larger.

Suddenly my shadow had become
that on a sidewalk at Hiroshima,
calling, "Why did you snatch my body? Why
did you steal what will be of no use to you?
We aren't the same size, didn't you know?"

The shadow and the sirens calling
and the fires continue to burn.

MILK RUN

Tokyo burning at nine o'clock.
We're heading north to Hokkaido.
Been on fire some time now,

wood and paper, uneven smoke piles,
snow on Fuji, imperfect sunrise.
Trapped like rats under collapsing frames.

Tell it to *Admiral* Tojo.

Squadron Double O peeling off,
headed west. Japan Sea.
"Let's play tag." That's my wingman,

the fool. "Nothing else to do." He
is right, of course. These missions
are a bore. How can I tell my boy

I knocked down zeroes when we
haven't seen one in months?
"Let's window shop. Down to 2, 1.5.

Waggle our wings. Why, I'll be Christ,
if they're not waving back."
Scuttlebutt has it, enemy suing

for peace. Seven more of these
milk runs and I can go home
sweet home. Hear we're gonna

drop a big one down south, maybe
something monster. Lots of hush, hush
about it. Enola Gay's off limits

past two weeks. Bundles of Dear Johns
every mail call. Lots of crews all shook up.
Not my worry, I don't think. I do

wish she'd learn to handle money better.
Oh, to see her face.

"Rendezvous for base return."
Gotta ditch the ord. No targets.
Can't take it back to Mama.

Our 'little war in the Pacific' may soon
be over, none too soon for me.

Boys that boasted, 'We'll be home
for Christmas,' forgot to say
which one.

THE OBCENITIES

of hate,
   rape,
   bomb,
   kill

all four
letter words

stop and
stop and
stop, too
as is
love

I need exponential language
words raised to the nth power
to explain how I feel
about what's coming down;
how else can I express dismay squared
or the cube of sorrow?

FOR THE RAINBOW WARRIOR*

You sailed for peace
into turbulent seas,
brash woman surrounded
by hostile men.

Green grow the rushes, ho!
Your fight with waves was not enough.
They had to shoot you down,
drop you in the deep, brash woman.

You were their conscience.
You reminded them too much
of their mothers
whom also they killed.

They blew you away
but you will blow back,
stronger, brasher still,
riding a victory wind.

---

*Blown up by French frogmen in a New Zealand harbor

THE BRIGHT LIGHT SEARCHES THE HEAVENS

They call it a new frontier
this place they are flying off to.
They want to see if *they* are there,
if something that looks like them
thinks like them, or even breathes.

They are so lonely, these white ones.
The volcano of Europe ejected them.
Like elephants they trample,
like moles they burrow,
like leeches they cling,
like jackals they deceive,
while the compulsion disease drives them
ever beyond what they've wasted,
toward their fantasy
of what is clean and new.

You must be born again.

Can we believe this dictum,
make it both cause and cure?

Come back, lost friends.
Eat apples, drink red wine,
make love, sit and conserve.

Autumn Is by Definition Wrinkled

Autumn is a trip gone haywire,
a standing order for sun,
color and falling leaves,

recipe for false summer,
fall sniffles,
babies conceived in January,
heartbreak.

Autumn too is definition.

Will the new friends
be like leaves, full
of flair, dash, flash
but fragile against
stiff winds?

Where are the birds of summer now?

Autumn signals Europe's harvest,
Asia's monsoons,
Zimbabwe heating up again.

Here, it is a time when old folks
gather their coats about them
and try to push back winter.

If He's Got the Time . . . .

Don't know if the medicine I am taking
supposed to cure me or keep me
from getting worse. Doctors never used to
tell you anything. Now they tell you so
much you can't make heads nor tails of it.
I gimp around on arthritic knees,
do my exercises in the pool.
Not the warm part, there's where
the old people are. Don't want
nothing to do with those old people.

Had to stop shopping on my bicycle. It
frightened my children, though
I bet my bones in better shape than theirs.

They've been *retired*. Someone's
beat them down, told them
they're no good for nothing. Let themselves
be boxed up in their "senior villages,"
"gray ghettos" — better consumer targets.

Sometimes I get so frustrated watching them,
I want to grab one by the shoulder
and shout, "Don't believe that hype!"
They'd put me away if I did that.

My kids wanted me in one of those
old folks refugee camps. "Mama you
need someone to help you with things.
You don't want to be alone."
(Translate: "We ain't got time to be bothered.")

House too big for you to care for
by yourself. (And we're not willing to drive
over once a month to help you clean it.)

They hounded me so that I got me
a tenant roomer. I met this artist
who runs a small uptown gallery.

One bit of talk led to another. Upshot
is, he's taken the attic and two rooms
on the top floor. Spent three weeks

schlepping all my stuff into the basement.
Lord, the things time loads you down with.
When she heard about it, my oldest daughter

pitched a fit. "You didn't consult with
the family." The family?
When the last time 'family' consulted
with me? I pay it no mind.

They're worried that he is younger than I am.
Well, what of it? I can take care of myself.
I finished high school when they still
taught you something.

He minds his business, I mine.
I have my reading circle, museum visits,
volunteer two days a month at the hospital.
I drive myself when I have to go too
far for the bus or commute train.

Now that we're settled, it's "Mama this"
or "Mama that." I pay it no mind.
Where were they when they thought I needed them?

My grandkids OK. Haven't picked up
their parents' greed; but TV's working at it.

Now as for my tenant/roomie/friend,
we eat together now and then.

I usually get prepared things from
the Chinese kitchen, or he'll do it.
I told him I've forgotten how to cook.
Then we might listen to music.
He seems to like my company,
I certainly do enjoy his.

My children are right, of course,
one thing can lead to another.
It's been six months. So far so good.
Occasionally there's a light in his eyes
that's more than spirit. Well,
if he's got the time, I've got the time.

ONE RESTLESS MOMENT

Rest, moment, let me look at you,
tenderly, for how beautiful you are
when dressed in autumn colors.

You, who will not wait,
who takes my day into night too early,
rest on this rock.

Blind, blind moment, so restless,
breaker of seasons with your breath,
let me count upon my fingers before
you sing coldly of winter.

KEEPING ON, WITH THANKS TO THE BARD

William S. says "shrunk shank,"
in reverence to a stage of loss.
Not that I'm in that kind of shrinkage yet;
though on some days I feel my entire
superstructure will 'dissolve into a dew.'

Those are dark times. Most days wax brighter.
Body steamed cleaned, salts washed down
with the fear. Sun shines, skies are clear.

Then there's the good good news day,
when life hits a peak and I'm ripe
for 'tomorrow and tomorrow and tomorrow.'